MEMOIR OF FATHER VINCENT DE PAUL

RELIGIOUS OF LA TRAPPE:
TRANSLATED FROM THE ORIGINAL FRENCH

by

A. M. POPE,

WITH A PREFACE

BY
THE RIGHT REVEREND DR. CAMERON,
BISHOP OF ARICHAT

First published in 1890

British Library Cataloguing-in-Publication Data
A catalogue record for this book is available
from the British Library

CONTENTS

PREFACE.

The reply of Maximilian to the wealthy courtier who tendered him a goodly purse of gold for a title of nobility, was worthy of that emperor: "I can enrich thee," he said, "but only thy own virtue can enoble thee" All true grandeur, excellence, and dignity, are the offspring of virtue. Even the most renowned oracles of paganism proclaim this, and the very persecutors of holiness are often constrained to pay homage to their victim. No wonder, then, that whenever we are privileged to find one of those rare mortals, whom virtue has unmistakably marked as her own, we lovingly attach an exceptional importance to everything connected with his history. Such assuredly was he whose "account of what befel" him during his first ten years in America, is now for the first time published in English. A brief sketch of the religious Order to which he belonged, of the life he led, and of the Monastery he founded, may give added interest to his own simple and edifying narrative.

What Scripture terms "the world," and so emphatically denounces as such, is the poisonous source of the mother-evils described by St. John as "the concupiscence of the flesh, and the concupiscence of the eyes, and the pride of life." Flight from the contamination of this threefold inordinate love of pleasures, riches and honors, being essential to salvation, is most easily, most surely and most meritoriously achieved by those who, in answer to a Divine call, consecrate and give themselves wholly to God, by the practice of the evangelical counsels of chastity, poverty and obedience. Those who embrace this angelic profession form the choice portion of the fold of Christ. They rank as His spouses, and, by the holy ambition of their virgin love, console Him for the craven defections or the cold indifference of so many Christians.

All Christians animated by the spirit of Jesus are religious, just as they are holy, and kings and priests (I Peter 2,9). Such is the unity of the marvellous body of Christ, the Church, whose soul is infinite love, that her every member shares, in some sense and measure, all her sublime prerogatives. But as God willed that in His family some goods should be common to all, so He likewise decreed that other goods should be reserved to comparatively few, and through these chosen and privileged ones benefit the rest. Hence, as besides this elementary royalty and priesthood conferred by baptism, there are, according to the express order of God superior and official royalties and priesthoods, in like manner besides the fundamental religion, which is the vital breath of every soul in a state of grace, there is a religion more eminent, more definite, more perfect. Thus as there is here below a sacerdotal and royal state, so likewise is there a religious state which is confined to those only who bind themselves by vows to a monastic life. It is evident, therefore, that when Catholics use the expression "religious Order," or term a monk or nun "a religious," they are perfectly justified in doing so, the cavillings of Dr. Trench to the contrary notwithstanding.

Each religious order is characterized by the special purpose for which it was founded, and by the constitution and rule which its members are to follow. The observance of the Benedictine rule was greatly relaxed in the monasteries of France towards the close of the eleventh century, when St. Robert (1098) inaugurated a reform at Citeaux, which resulted in the establishment of the Cistercian Order. A monastery of this Order was subsequently (1140) founded in La Perche, France, by the Count of Perche, and was called La Trappe. In 1662 the commendatory abbot of

La Trappe, Armand Jean le Bouthilier de Rance', a nobleman who abandoned wealth and a brilliant career, visited La Trappe, undertook a new reform of the Cistercian rule, and thus became the founder of that branch of this Order which became known as the congregation of La Trappe. In consequence of the Revolution of 1789, one of the Trappist Fathers, Dom Augustin conducted twenty-four of his brethren from France to Valsainte, in Switzerland. Here they decided to adopt a rule still more strict than that which they had hitherto observed. This step occasioned a division in the Trappist Order: some monasteries following the rule of Valsainte, others that of de Rance'. An appeal to Rome resulted in a decree dated October 3rd, 1834, by which all Trappist monasteries were placed under one government. The decree not having however had the desired effect, the Holy See decided in 1847 to sanction two distinct congregations, one to follow the constitution of de Rance', and the other to observe the rule of St. Benedict, with the primitive constitution of the Cistercian Order. To the latter congregation belong the Trappist monasteries of Canada and the United States, whose time-table on week days during winter is as follows:—

At two o'clock, a. m., the Trappists rise and proceed to their chapel, where they devote their time to the recitation of the Office, meditation, &c., till 7.45, when they have High Mass, followed by manual labor, which, with the interruption of only half an hour given to the recitation of Office and examen of conscience, continues till 2 p. m.; ten minutes more and they break their long fast of twenty-four hours with the lean and only repast of the day. At 6 p. m. begins spiritual reading, immediately followed by compline and other devotional exercises till 7, when they retire to their much needed rest on their hard straw mattresses. Perpetual silence is prescribed, unless in case of necessity, so that the Trappist's whole life is one of extraordinary austerity and of incessant recollection, reminding him at every turn of the shortness of life and the tremendous rigor of judgment. The time-table for summer varies in some minor practices and observances, while, according to that of Sundays and holidays, those religious in the latter case rise at midnight, and in the former at 1 a. m., and busy themselves till 7 o'clock, p. m. during winter, and 8 o'clock during summer in the praises of the Lord.

James Merle was born at Lyons, France, the 29th October, 1768. His father was a much respected physician in that city. On the 7th of April, 1798, while the godless Revolution was carrying resistless devastation over the country, he privately received the holy order of priesthood at the hands of Mgr. C. F. D. Dubois de Sanzay, Archbishop of Vienne, and seven years afterwards he entered the Trappist Order, taking the name of Father Vincent de Paul, by which he has always since been known.

In his memoir Father Vincent speaks of having bought a large tract of land near the sea in Nova Scotia, and of having built a house thereon. This was in Tracadie, where he resided for some years previous to his return to France in 1823. In 1824 he came again to Tracadie with another worthy priest of his Order, Father Francis, a native of Freiburg, together with three lay brothers, and the house above referred to became thenceforth the monastery of Petit Clairvaux. A few years later three other lay brothers were admitted, two of them from Halifax, and one from the United States.

Until the Rev. John Quinn was appointed parish priest of Tracadie, (1837) Father Vincent had pastoral charge of the three missions of Tracadie, Havre au Boucher, and Pomquet, and the old people of the place still recount his innumerable acts of extraordinary zeal and devotion. "He scarcely ever had the stole off his neck during Lent," is the remark of one of them. He also made frequent excursions to Cheticamp, Arichat, and other parts of Cape Breton, to preach missions there, and to assist the dying. In his memoir he speaks of that sublime pilgrimage of the heart, the admirable devotion of the Way of the Cross, as one especially acceptable to God; and no wonder it bore marvellous fruit as conducted by him. At each station this holy servant of God did not content himself with reading the usual prayers:

he gave expression to heavenly thoughts inspired by his own burning love of his crucified Saviour, producing a mysterious and lasting echo in all hearts. The church was always crowded on those occasions. To prepare children for their first communion, he devoted six entire weeks of instruction each year. His capacity for work was immense; and while hurry never appeared in his actions, he managed to glide through them with a masterly ease far out-stripping the speediest progress of ordinary mortals. A supernatural light seemed to supersede the necessity of recourse to the usual slow and laborious process of reasoning in seeing one's way, and to endow him with an intuition excluding all doubt, and with an instinct ever ready in performance. Thus for everything he found ample time, because no particle of his time was lost. He was a living, palpitating, breathing, vocal, acting temple of the Holy Ghost, and this Divine indwelling was, in a manner, visible to all. At the altar, during the holy sacrifice which he daily offered, it seemed to transfigure his countenance so as to impress his heavenly citizenship upon all beholders. In administering the sacrament, in instructing the people, in his incessant endeavors to keep or win them from sin, and to provide for all their spiritual wants, the same irradiation of holiness imparted the most extraordinary efficacy to his charity and zeal.

So palpable was this impress of sanctity in his every-day-life, that no one could come in contact with him without perceiving it and feeling its inherent power. Such being the rare effulgence of Father Vincent's sanctity as seen amid the dust and darkness of the world, one can more readily realize the transcendent perfection and purity of his soul as nurtured and revealed in his divine communing in his own beloved cloister. No wonder, then, that when this admirable servant of God, fall of days and merits, was called away to his reward on the morning of New Year's Day, 1853, all felt that they had one intercessor more in heaven. No wonder that miraculous cures wrought through his mediation began soon to multiply. Nor was Father Vincent's reputation for sanctity confined to Catholics. Even Protestants not only acknowledged the heroism of his virtues, but also sought to possess some earth from his grave, and one of them, J. H., still living, was restored to health and usefulness by the application of this relic to his diseased and disabled limbs.

The next Prior of Petit Clairvaux was the dauntless and holy Father Francis, whose advanced age obliged him in 1858 to resign his office into the hands of the sweet Father James, a native of Belgium, and a religious eminently qualified for the position. Such was the success of his administration that in 1876 the community was raised by Pius IX of blessed memory to the dignity of an abbey—an abbey, which, with its forty-one fervent religious, now wisely governed by the worthy Abbot Dominic, presents an example of heroic abstinence, mortification and prayer, well calculated to put the characteristic dissipation, effeminacy and dissoluteness of the age to blush, and to bring home to our minds that "the wisdom of this world is foolishness with God." (I Co. 3,19).

JOHN CAMERON, *Bishop of Arichat.*

MEMOIR OF FATHER VINCENT.

[Some account of what befel Father Vincent de Paul, Religious of La Trappe, with observations made by him when in America, where he has spent about ten years, with the permission of his Superior, in obedience to whose orders he writes the following:]

The reverend Father Abbot, of La Trappe, Dom Augustin, (De Lestrange) foreseeing that Bonaparte would seek to destroy the communities existing in Europe, resolved on sending a party of his religious to America, in order that they might establish themselves there and preserve their monastic state.

In 1812, I, in company with two other brothers, was sent by him to the United States, there to found an establishment of our Order. We left Bordeaux on the 15th June, and on the 6th of the month of August we arrived at Boston. We had with us one of our Trappistines, whose object was also to found a community; with this intention she had preceded her companions, but now found herself alone, as passports were refused to the other sisters. We were welcomed by the worthy Mr. Matignon, parish priest of the town, who coaxed us to remain in the diocese of Bishop Cheverus. However as we had received orders to establish ourselves near Baltimore, after a few days rest I started for that town alone, leaving my brothers and the nun in Boston, intending to send for them when I should find a suitable site for the two projected establishments. I paid my respects to His Grace the Archbishop of Baltimore, who received me kindly, but appeared at a loss where to find a site such as we desired. After many unsuccessful efforts and researches, he established me temporally on a farm belonging to the Society of Jesus (of which he was a member) until such time as we could procure the sort of place we wanted; then as I thought that time might be long in coming, I summoned my brothers to me, and arranged for a suitable lodging for the nun.

11

During our stay, a rich man of Baltimore, who was once a Protestant and had been converted, offered us 2000 acres of land in the mountains of Pensylvania, near a river called the Delaware. He was even generous enough to offer me the services of his son, who was also a recent convert, and who came with us to point out the property which, however, I was not able to inspect thoroughly as I remained there only one day.

I returned soon after with two young men who were inclined to join our Order. They commenced a somewhat rude novitiate, for we fasted and kept silence on the way, going always on foot for want of money. After great suffering from fatigue and heat (as it was summer), we arrived at a little town, distant about sixty miles from Philadelphia, whence we had started on our tour of inspection. This little town, which was called Milford, was quite near to the land that was to be ours.

On the way we passed through many Protestant villages whose inhabitants appeared to be anxious for the light of the true faith, and this budding town of Milford did not look askance at us, as almost all of its inhabitants came to mass on Sunday. After mass one of the young men aforementioned, who knew English well, expounded the catechism to them, and they listened with attention. The Protestant minister came afterwards to preach, but we were told that none of the people went to hear him which without doubt annoyed him greatly. One of the principal men of the place, a Protestant, as indeed they were all, begged me to remain with them, saying that they would subscribe me a pension, and that he would head the list with the sum of fifty dollars. But we had not come to this country to be missionaries, so we left Milford to go and inspect our land.

Travelling through these immense and trackless forests was very difficult, and we often went astray. One day when I was alone with a child who served me in the capacity of guide, we were greatly puzzled. We wished to find a little hut that we had built in the woods in which to sleep; nightfall was coming on, and there seemed no chance of finding our camp before sundown. I said to the child: "here is a low, flat rock, on which I will spend the night." He replied that if I remained there I should be devoured by the bears, of which there were a great number on these mountains; we had already heard their cries and hideous howlings. At length, thanks be to God, we found the cabin, which was not a very safe refuge for us, as it was only a little hut built of young trees. The two novices and I slept there like Indians, either on the bare ground or on couches formed by heaps of the branches of trees.

Having no provisions with us we were obliged for the first few days to eat what we could find in the woods, such as certain little blue berries that they call "bluets," and other wild fruits, which the people of the country despise. On the third or fourth day help came. A Jew and a Protestant appeared on the scene, bringing us potatoes. This Jew showed a leaning towards our religion, and the Sunday previous I had said mass in his house. I do not doubt that if we had remained longer with these people many would have been converted. There was one entire family, of father, mother and three children, whom I had instructed, and who were to receive baptism and embrace the Catholic religion. Unfortunately the woman was the victim of evil counsel at Milford, and was deterred from her good purpose. There were many people in Milford who were bitter enemies to the truth.

I often said mass in our cabin. One day we made a cross and carried it in procession for nearly a mile: we sang psalms, and part of the way went barefoot, until we reached the spot where we planted the cross, which was our consolation and our safeguard, as there were in this desert a great number of rattlesnakes and other reptiles no less dangerous. When we left our retreat we would sometimes step upon them and would hear the noise that these serpents make with their rattles.

At last having walked over a great portion of these two thousand acres of land during the two weeks that we spent there, we left these solitudes and went down to Philadelphia. [Footnote: It was not deemed advisable to accept this property, it being almost entirely rock or marsh land. Besides which it was not suitable for one of our establishments, communication with other places being too difficult.]

Upon arriving at the town I told the Bishop how well-disposed were the people whom we had seen, and suggested to him to send some missionaries there, but he told me that he had none to send. If I had been free I would have returned at once to labor for the conversion of these poor people.

After a year of crosses and difficulties in the way of our discovering a suitable and convenient place for our establishment, we found ourselves in Maryland, an excellent province, producing all the necessaries of life in abundance. It is near the sea, and near to the Potoxen, and not far from the Potomac, two great rivers that add to its commercial advantages and render it more flourishing. We thought we had at last found the country in which to succeed in establishing our foundation. I consulted His Grace the Archbishop of Baltimore, and the reverend gentlemen of the seminary of St. Sulpice, and in accordance with their advice, I decided to go there and commence the work. Three more brothers sent from France by our Reverend Father Abbot, arrived at this juncture and joined us. We bought the land and set ourselves to work to cultivate it. We built a house for ourselves, which consisted of trees placed one upon another—what is called in this country a loghouse. It was small, being only eighteen feet long, and as many wide. We shortly commenced another which would serve as a chapel. The negroes of the country—who are all Catholics—gave us a helping hand in this work On arriving here we found lodgings in a private house near our clearing, in which we remained until our loghouse was fit to receive us.

Maryland produces an abundance of Indian corn, the cultivation of which is the chief work of the negroes. We subsisted almost entirely upon this food, with potatoes and occasionally bread; wheat, however, and buckwheat grow very well. We arrived there at the beginning of the year 1813, and during the winter we were occupied in cutting down trees and preparing the land for work in the spring, so that when that season arrived we had an acre and a half of land under cultivation. Part of this we planted with potatoes, another part was a garden where we sowed different vegetables, and we also laid out an orchard of young fruit trees. So far everything looked well, but when summer came, and while we were working most zealously we all fell ill with fever, and many of us were attacked with dysentery. I attribute these maladies to many causes,—first to the miasma or poisonous vapors exhaled from newly cleared land, then to the great heat and the bad water that we had to drink, which, though it had been pure enough in the winter and spring, had become bad by reason of a multitude of little insects that were perpetually drowning themselves in it. Another reason that contributed to render us ill was the number of different sorts of flies by which we were devoured day and night. There were among others two species of flies which in this country they call tics. Some of them are large, others are small, they fasten themselves to the skin and so penetrate into the flesh that one can only remove them by pulling them to pieces, even then a part remains and causes an insupportable itching.

We were dying one after another in this place when our Rev. Father Abbot on his way from Martinique, with several religious, arrived at New York. He summoned our community to him, as well as that of the Rev. Father Urbain, which a short time previously had united with ours, so that these three little communities now formed but one, under our chief Superior, who thus in a moment effected a foundation such as we had spent years of fruitless effort endeavoring to establish. Our new monastery was established in the country near New York, and did much good. Thirty-three poor children (almost all of them orphans) were brought up there, and were given all the necessaries of life, even to their clothes. Protestants came to see the good work and two ministers were converted. These gentlemen came sometimes to see us, and assisted at our religious ceremonies. They liked to converse with our Reverend Father Abbot, who won them by his frank and polite manner. In addition to the work of this monastery, our Reverend Father Abbot supported and directed another house of our Order which he had also founded, and which was productive of much good. This was a community of nuns. There was yet another convent, one belonging to the Ursulines quite near, that is to say about three or four miles from our monastery, which our community supplied with a chaplain. I was obliged to go there every Sunday to say mass and to confess the nuns. When we arrived in their neighborhood they were without a priest; we could not leave them in such need, so that I, ill though I was, had to say two masses on Sundays, one in the church of the Ursulines, the other in that of our sisters. However, this was to me a cause of rejoicing, although I was fatigued after my voyages and overwhelmed by the work with which I was charged, I was compensated and consoled by the good that I could be the means of doing. I remember having received the abjuration of Protestantism of three young ladies who were boarders at the Ursuline Convent, and who had the happiness of becoming Catholics.

Although we were in a Protestant country, our Reverend Father Abbot undertook to have the procession of the Blessed Sacrament on the festival of Corpus Christi, thinking it might do some good. He had several repositories built in a field adjoining our house, these he decorated in the best style possible and managed to have a canopy and boys to swing censors and others to throw flowers before the Blessed Sacrament. When the time for the procession arrived we saw our Reverend Father bearing Jesus Christ in his hands and walking under the dais borne by four religious in dalmatics accompanied by the community and by several strangers singing hymns and canticles. Numbers of children preceeded the Blessed Sacrament, exercising the solemn functions which had been allotted to them. This infantine band, clad in white surplices girded with different colors, resembled angels and presented a spectacle at once beautiful and edifying to the beholder. The Protestants who were present appeared to be much pleased with the procession.

Our Reverend Father Abbot wished with all his heart to be able to continue the good work thus commenced, but he was obliged to abandon it for want of pecuniary means, and perhaps also because of the ill-will of many who offered opposition to his projects; besides which King Louis XVIII had been restored to the throne of France, and religion was being re-established in that country. Almost all our brothers were dispersed here and there throughout Europe, and it would be necessary to reunite them. Persuaded, besides, that he would receive more help in France than in the United States, and in short, reflecting that there would perhaps be more good to be done yet in the old world than in the new, (the Revolution having been the cause of such wickedness and having done so much harm) our Father Abbot decided that he and his community would return to France. He embarked in the autumn of 1814, and took with him from New York the greater number of our Brothers and all our Sisters, leaving only six Brothers and myself behind, with orders that we should join him in France after I had arranged our business matters and recovered my strength, for I had still within me the germ of that malady of which mention has been made in speaking of Maryland where I contracted it, as did the others. It left me with a slow fever, that lasted for a long time.

At this junction two of our Brothers died, a lay Brother and an oblate. This latter had been almost a millionaire he having acquired a large fortune in the West India Islands; he lost it, however, in the negro rebellion, and retired to La Trappe, where he died poor enough.

Belonging to the house in which we were living was an orchard which we had made our cemetery, here we had buried our two brothers; but, as we were going to leave this spot and did not wish to expose their bodies to be perhaps profaned by heretics who might buy the ground and not wish to have them there, we determined to exhume them. They had been buried about a fortnight, and the weather was warm, so we provided ourselves with incense to burn in case there might be a foul odour. This precaution, however, was not necessary, as there was no smell perceptible, they were as fresh, so to speak, as if they were still alive. We remarked especially that the body of Brother Jean Marie, (the lay Brother) was supple. I touched it myself, and saw that it was really so, for while I held him his legs swayed as would those of a person in life.

Near the town there was a little cemetery well walled in, and intended for the poor. As our brothers were poor in fact, and by profession, I had them laid there, and in the same spirit of poverty interred them side by side in the same grave. We accompanied these good brothers to the tomb, offering our prayers for their repose, and all was finished before daylight.

About the middle of the month of May, 1815, our business being concluded, we left New York, and fifteen days later arrived at Halifax, without having experienced bad weather. After two week's delay in searching for another vessel, we at length found one, and by means of the recommendation of Mr. Burke, then pastor of the town, and since Bishop, we were taken on board with our seven trunks without being obliged to pay anything for our passage. The ship was a transport called the "Ceylon," and was delayed by contrary winds. The second day after we embarked the wind still being from a wrong quarter, I was stupid and imprudent enough to go ashore to see about some business that was not of grave importance—when lo! the wind veered round suddenly and became favorable. The ship sailed, but Father, Vincent remained and lost his passage!

I thus found myself alone in a strange country, and without means. I made every effort to discover some way of overtaking the ship, but in vain. It was impossible to do so, and I felt very sad at the thought of my brothers being carried so far away from me.

My Superior in France, to whom I made known this event, wrote to me that as God had permitted it, I could remain until farther orders, and occupy myself with the salvation of the Indians; for which object I accordingly labored up to the time of my leaving Nova Scotia, that is to say up to the month of October,

1823. These labors, however, did not prevent my working for the good of our Order, as we shall see later.

Mr. Bourke having gone to Ireland, we were only two priests for the town of Halifax and its suburbs, where there were many Catholics, without counting the Mic-macs, who are the Indians inhabiting Nova Scotia. These Indians were called to the Faith about four centuries ago. French priests or Jesuits coming at the peril of their lives, brought them the light of the Gospel. Many of these ministers of our Lord fell victims of their own zeal and charity, being murdered by this nation, then pagan and barbarous. Since these Indians became acquainted with the true religion they have never been known to conform to any other, but have preserved their firmness in the faith up to the present day in spite of the danger of perversion to which they are so often exposed, more especially since they have lived among the English, and in spite of their ignorance, for it is difficult to teach them. Their language which they call "Mic-mac," is a jargon without rule. They have been taught to read in it, but only by means of hieroglyphics. A figure or a sign which they write themselves on bark or on paper, may sometimes signify only one word, sometimes again it stands for a whole phrase. Some have thought they detected Arab words amongst this language, but I think it bears more resemblance to that of children just learning to speak without being able to understand what they say. For example for the "yes" they say [long-e] (ay); for "no" they say "mena." The accent of the Mic-mac is soft and slow. I have remarked that, they do not convey their ideas well in any other language. When one translates Mic-mac for them into French or English, they often appear dissatisfied, and one can see from their manner that the true sense is not given. What renders their faith more remarkable and meritorious is, that they confess through the medium of an interpreter, and they avail themselves of the first they find, no matter who, provided he knows their language. They are often interpreted by their relatives, even the oldest by the youngest. Mr. Mayar, a French priest who was formerly missionary to these parts and who died in Halifax full of merit before God, was deeply regretted by these Indians. By means of great application, and by the aid of light from heaven, he accomplished the task of translating into their language a number of the prayers and chants of the church, so that they now sing the Kyrie, the Gloria in Excelsis, the Credo, &c, even the Te Deum, on the Roman or Parisian tone, (for this worthy priest came from Paris). They know many hymns of the Blessed Virgin, which they sing equally well, also the prose Dies Irae. They sing mass fairly well, especially the tone Royal, and the mass for the dead. Some persons may be surprised at this, and perhaps harbor a doubt of it, but I can testify as a witness to its truth. More than a hundred times they have sung it for me. So recently as the month of August, 1823, I was in a parish called Havre-a-Bouchers, when twenty-six canoes filled with Indians arrived there; they came to have their children baptised, and for confession, &c. There were eight singers among them, and during the week that they remained, they sang mass for me each day, and one might say conducted themselves like canons or like Trappists! They have clear voices. These poor Indians might shame some of our European Catholics by their zeal and their piety; they will go fifty or even a hundred leagues to find a priest and to receive the Sacraments, and as it often happens that they have no provisions when they arrive, they pass two or three days without eating, occupied only with their souls and forgetful of the wants of the body.

While in Halifax, which is the capital of Nova Scotia, I found myself overladen with work. The priest who was with me being in very delicate health and often indisposed, most of the work fell to me. He was at length obliged to go away for change of air and was absent for a month, during which time it fell to me to baptize, confess, marry, visit the sick in town and country, and be on my feet day and night, besides saying mass on Sundays and Holy days.

Although I knew very little English, I preached twice in that language in the Catholic church of the town, where there were about two thousand Catholics, of whom the greater number were Irish.

Soon I felt constrained to go further into the Province of Nova Scotia to minister to the wants of the poor, neglected inhabitants. The first place to which I went was a parish called Chezzetcook, composed of French Acadians, who were without a priest. It is seven leagues from the town (Halifax) and when it possessed a missionary the Indians had been accustomed to go there. They were not long in learning of my presence, and came from a circuit of fifteen or twenty leagues. I had a transparancy representing the suffering souls in purgatory, which our Revered Father Abbot had made. The figures expressing different shades of grief and of the desire as well as the hope of seeing God, combined with the brilliant and real looking flames, were well calculated to produce an impression. I showed it to them and explained it by means of one of their interpreters who knew French. At once penetrated with compassion and charity for the suffering souls in purgatory they began to weep, and to look up the money they had with them so as to have the Holy Sacrifice offered on behalf of these suffering souls, and that without my having said anything to give them the idea. They all wear the cross, some have it hung round their necks, others fasten it on their breast. It is seldom that an Indian leaves home without his beads; they generally have them and do not neglect to say them, sometimes repeating the chapelet several times a day, as well as in the middle of the night, when they rise to pray. They observe all the fasts of the Church, and the penances imposed on them they generally perform on Fridays. On that day in a spirit of penitence, and in memory of the passion of Jesus Christ, a man will hold out to his wife the backs of his hands, which the wife strikes with a rod, giving twenty, thirty, or fifty blows. She then in turn presents her hands and receives the same chastisement from her husband. This chastisement is dealt out indiscriminately, children are thus chastized by their parents, and what is surprising, the little Indians when struck on the hands do not withdraw them, no matter how much they feel the pain. I have seen them bleeding, yet in spite of that they were firm and motionless. Their religion is not only exterior, they have it in their heart as will be seen by the following fact: The feast of St. Anne is a great festival for the Indians, and I made a point of being at Chezzetcook on that day. Two hundred Indians assembled, most of them came in a spirit of devotion, but some of them had evil designs, for they mediated killing their king and all his family. I discovered this plot in time, and learnt the cause with astonishment. It was that they believed that the chief and all his family would change their religion, that they had become Protestants, or that they intended so to do. This is how it came about. Some heretics called Methodists, had done all in their power to attract the king of the Indians to their sect, going so far as to give him all sorts of provisions, and other valuables, such as cows, pigs, farming implements, &c. One of these Methodists was sent among the Indians to learn their language, and so corrupt them more easily. In this way the report got about that their Chief, Benjamin (which was the name of the king) had joined the Methodists with all his family. Mr. Mignault, parish priest of Halifax, and myself knew this to be false, for Benjamin himself, whom we had warned against the dangers that threatened him, had replied: "The potatoes, cows, and the other provisions of Bromlet (which was the name of the Methodist who had given him the things) are good, I have taken them and made use of them, but his religion is worthless, I will have none of it."

In consequence of this we assembled the Indians in the church of Chezztecook, which was not large enough to hold them all, and we made the king repeat his profession of faith in their presence, so that they should no longer doubt his sincerity. He did this in a most edifying manner. His example was followed by all his officers, who also made their profession of faith. We remarked in particular one of his brothers who was conspicuous by the touching beauty and eloquence of his speech, and by the earnestness of the gestures which he employed. Some fragments of his discourse were rendered into our language by an Acadian interpreter, who understood Mic-mac pretty well.

"How," said he, "could we leave our religion that will save our souls if we follow it, this religion that comes from God, whose son died on the cross for our salvation? Shall we lose our souls that have cost Him so dear, for which he suffered so much, and which he shed all his blood to purchase? No, better die than change our faith and do such a great wrong."

I had written to Mr. Mignault to come so as to render the affair more imposing and dignified, and he arrived in good time. He carried a large crucifix, which at the conclusion of the ceremony the Indians came to venerate. The missionary then said a few words of instruction, after which the Indians embraced each other as brothers and friends, in token of general satisfaction and peace. I heard all their confessions, and a large number had the happiness of receiving Holy Communion. On the eve of St. Anne's feast, they made a bonfire, and while the wood burned they fired off guns and danced around the fire, clapping their hands in imitation of musical instruments. This lasted for a great part of the night, however, they had previously said their evening prayers, and sung hymns and canticles.

We can obtain almost anything from them in the name of our holy religion, so great is their attachment to it, as will be seen by the following: One day while I was in Halifax, a number of Indians came to the presbytery to complain to me of the Governor who resided in the town. They clamored for the guns and powder which had been promised to them, and which they were accustomed to receive every year from the English Government in addition to their gifts of woolen blankets. The missionaries distributed, or saw to the distribution of these latter. I was obliged to go myself to see the Governor on the subject of this small rebellion, for the Indians wore a threatening air. His Excellency begged me to pacify them and to tell them that their demand would soon be granted. I returned and said a few words in the name of religion, which at once quieted them.

Another time some barbarous and fanatical miscreants set a

number of Indians against us, making them believe that we only drew them around us in order to do them harm, and to emperil their safety. This they apparently believed, for we were warned that they would attempt our lives. I spoke to them instructing them as well as I was able. At last by the arguments of the religion to which they are so attached, I turned them from their wicked purpose. I am sure that afterwards they experienced a lively remorse for having entertained such a thought. Formerly, that is to say, before priests came among them, they had the barbarous custom of killing their fathers and mothers when they became old and infirm. Many of the bludgeons and war clubs with which they killed their parents have been found quite recently. Now, however, they take care of them until their death, respecting and loving them. It is thought that before they had any knowledge of religion they were cannibals.

How is it that this people who were formerly so unnatural and so barbarous are to-day so different, so humane, and quiet and tractible? What has rendered them so docile and submissive; in short, what has worked this happy change if not the Catholic religion? Protestants, as we have shown above, have tried to civilize them, and to imbue them with different sentiments, even going so far as to live among them and entering into their pursuits, but their undertakings have always failed, each attempt has met with the same result It is only the true religion and its priests that have power to convert and civilize these savages and make them useful members of society. Each year they have masses said for different intentions, and in this they give evidence of generosity and nobleness of sentiment. The first mass that they recommend is for the human race, that is for all men living; the second is for the souls in purgatory; the third for all Indians and others who have died during the year; the fourth to thank God for all benefits received from His hand during the year, and the fifth to offer up to Him the coming year so that he may bless it. For this object they save their money, sometimes to the end of the year, sometimes to the feast of St. Anne, when they have an opportunity to come to their religious duties. This, however, does not prevent their having a special mass said, should any of their near relatives die. They generally recommend high masses for these general intentions, and for thanksgiving.

Before the French took possession of Nova Scotia, which they called Acadia, the Indians lived only by hunting and fishing, and had no clothing, but such as they made of the skins of wild beasts. Their houses were hut-like in form, as they are at the present time, for they have not changed their ancient manner of living. I have often slept in their cabins, which are very uncomfortable for civilized people, such as Frenchmen, although the Indians prefer them to our houses. A proof of this is that, notwithstanding the length of time they have lived among Europeans, they have not made up their mind to imitate them. This may possibly arise from idleness, for it would cost them much labor as well as time and money were they to erect houses such as ours. They are not rich enough to employ workmen, but in less than a day, without expense and with little labor, they can build the house in which they live, sleep, cook, &c., and which is much less trouble for them. They cut fifteen or twenty little trees of about the same size as the arm of a youth of fifteen. From these they remove the branches, if there be any, and make them into posts of nine or ten feet in length. They then plant them in the earth at equal distances, in the form of a circle, placing them so that they may incline inwards, so that the base is much larger than the summit. An opening is left at the apex sufficient to admit of the escape of the smoke from the fire, which is always made in the middle of the cabin. They then cover these poles with the bark of trees, leaving an open space for the entrance. If they are not too poor, they cover this space with some pieces of old blankets. Their houses are built in the shape of a sugar loaf, their bed is the naked earth, or some small branches of trees, shreded fine, that serve as a mattrass. These cabins are never more than fifteen or twenty feet in diameter.

Their cookery consists chiefly in suspending above their fire some eels or hares that they have killed. These they eat almost before they have changed color, (what the Acadians term boucare). There are some who have kettles, and who cook their fish in water, with potatoes, which vegetable for some time past the Indians of Nova Scotia have planted, and which now forms almost their principle nourishment. Many have boats in which they go codfishing. Although they are generally rather idle, they occupy themselves nevertheless at work which requires attention and a certain kind of application, such as making pretty boats out of bark and pretty boxes of different shapes and colors, and elegant and highly ornamented baskets. For this ornamentation they use the quills of the porcupine, an animal very common in America. These quills they die black, red, blue, &c. They make these colors themselves by means of certain barks which they boil in water. They then fasten the colored quills on the bark of their boxes in tasteful and varied patterns. This is generally considered to be women's work. That of the men is heavier, such as the making of churns and other wooden utensils for domestic use. They tan the skins of the animals they kill and make their shoes or moccasins out of them. These are very thin and do not last long. As, regards their dress, both men and women are oddly attired. Their clothes are fashioned somewhat after the manner of ours, but the sewing is all on the outside and the stitches are very large. The selvedge of the cloth, (which they are always careful to secure when buying it) also shews on the outside, from their shoulders to their heels, and is considered ornamental. The squaws' dresses are similar, with the addition of a hood, which, when turned up, completely covers their head. The more elegant are ornamented with ribbons, flowers, beads, &c. It is more particularly when they come to their devotions that they decorate themselves thus. The men also at such times dress themselves with more than usual care. They live very peaceably together, willingly lend to each other, and have almost everything in common. If one receives a gift of anything, bread for example, all the others, men and women, regard it as a present made to all, and are as grateful as if each had received it, consequently there is no such thing as jealousy among them. A beautiful example for all Christians!

We will now speak of their dexterity. It is wonderful to see them manage their bark canoes, which are extremely light. These little boats are narrow at both ends, a little wider in the middle, and generally about nine or ten feet long. They move with surprising quickness in the midst of the angry waves. Two persons are sufficient to propel them, and it can be done by one. When fishing eels they stand at the end of their canoes and spear the eels with a long stick, to the end of which is fastened a sharp pointed iron. This instrument they call higogue. They are so long sighted that they can see to the bottom, of water twenty feet in depth. They wait until the fish rise, then spear them as they go along. Their dexterity is such that they seldom miss their aim. I have often gone with them; we have journeyed together by sea and by land. When there are portages, that is to say lands to cross, in order to regain the sea or lakes, they put their canoes on their heads and carry them to the water, and if they are overtaken by rain or by bad weather, they turn them over and take shelter underneath them.

Without counting the Indians who in 1818 numbered many thousand souls in Nova Scotia and in Cape Breton, which Province alone, is almost as large as France, there were at least twelve hundred and fifty Catholic families scattered over these two large Provinces. At that time we numbered only seven priests, two of whom were very infirm, which was the reason of my being obliged to leave the Halifax mission and to repair to a place two hundred miles from there, on the coast of the Gulf of St. Lawrence, and in the neighborhood of Cape Breton, This part of Nova Scotia (to which I was sent by Bishop Burke on his return from his visit to Europe, where he had been made Bishop of Sion and Vicar Apostolic of this Province), was without a priest, although it contained a great number of Catholics. On my arrival I found three parishes abandoned and deprived of the precious consolations of religion. Many children were brought to me for baptism, and I had numerous confessions to hear, &c. They came from great distances to take me to visit the sick who had ample time to die before I could get near them.

I was given especial charge of three parishes composed of Acadians and of natives of France, to whom the English Government had given land, and who still remain in this country. The Acadian portion of my charge having intermarried with the Indians, had become half savage, and had adopted many of the Indian customs. [Footnote: Le peuple Acadien s'etant allie avec les Sauvages, est devenu moitie Sauvage, et a pris beaucoup de leurs manieres.] There is a tribe of the Indians called Micmacs in one of these three parishes that is named Pomquet (an Indian word) and I was in a position to observe them as they were only ten miles from Tracadie, which was my ordinary place of residence. They there possessed a considerable property given to them by the Government. They cultivated it, planted potatoes and cut hay. When I arrived among them I found great disorder. Many had given themselves up to drunkeness, and they were without a chief. One day I assembled them together and spoke to them strongly about these matters. Since then I have seen with pleasure that they have not opposed me, but that they have chosen among themselves a chief whom they obey,—not all of them unfortunately, for there are some of them who are wicked and have always given me much trouble; their love for brandy is their ruin.

I have often crossed an arm of the sea in order to visit other Micmacs who live in Cape Breton. This Cape is surrounded by little islands, and there is there a lake seven leagues in length and five or six in width; on which I was once shipwrecked. We were two priests in a bark canoe, paddled by two Indians, and were carrying the consolations of religion to many families of Indians who lived on the other side at the foot of a mountain. A storm suddenly arose, a long stick, which served as a mast and carried a sail, was broken, and during the two hours that the bad weather continued, we momentarily expected to be engulfed by the immense waves that rose like hills and fell, breaking against our feeble bark, although the pilot endeavored to avoid them as much as possible, while the other Indian tried to break their force by means of his paddle. One of these Indians, the elder of the two, and the more experienced, trembled, fearing every moment that we should be lost, and he was not so afraid for us as we were for ourselves. However, thanks to Providence, and to the wood of the True Cross that I had with me, we were delivered from danger, and arrived safely in port.

We found a new plantation made by the Indians, that is to say, some tracts of cultivated land, some animals and some frames of houses. The Indians received us with great joy, especially when they learned that we were two priests who came to visit them; but in nearing their habitations we were exposed to great danger from the horns of a bull that was ferocious and was in the habit of rushing at passers by. God delivered us from this peril also, although the animal in question was quite near to us.

These Indians set before us for our supper, tea, milk, butter, potatoes and some fruit that resembled small apples (petites pommes). We were hungry and tired. We ate with good appetites, and were anxious to retire for the night. But what beds! Appropriate truly for a Trappist. They were made of grass and of branches of trees thrown on the ground. And what a house! It had no chimney and scarcely any roof, so that we were all night exposed to the snow and rain which was falling. My companion who was suffering from lung complaint was injured by this, while for my part, I shivered all night and could not get warm, although quite near to a fire that had been kindled in the centre of the cabin.

The next morning we rose before daybreak and baptized several Micmac children, (for these Indians were of the same nation as those of Nova Scotia) and confessed others. After that we prepared to re-cross the lake, which was not easy, as the sea was still very high.

Another time that I started on a mission to this same Cape (Breton) the Indians who conducted me in a canoe perceived three monstrous fish called maraches, and they were frightened, as these fish are very dangerous. Their teeth are made like gardiners' knives, for cutting and boring, or like razors slightly bent. They are extremely voracious, and often follow boats, attacking them with violence. Bark canoes cannot resist them, they rend them open with their teeth, so that they sink to the bottom, which is why the Indians have such a terror of them. Happily for us these fish did not follow us, we arrived, thank God, in good health.

Tracadie was usually my starting place when I left for the Indian mission of Cape Breton. I had from eighteen to twenty leagues to journey by water, making long circuits and paddling round twelve or fifteen little islands, and passing near many others. Nevertheless it only takes one day to make the journey in a bark canoe, that is if the wind be not contrary. The Micmacs of the Cape (Breton) knowing that I was on the road and would soon arrive at the mission [Footnote: This place is called "Mission" or "The Mission of the Bras d'or," because it is there that the missionaries are accustomed to confess, baptize and administer the Sacraments to the Indians, and to those who present themselves to receive them. It is a pretty little island on which they have built a nice chapel, and a house sufficiently commodious for the priest.] would all gather there to the number of five or six hundred. On the occasion referred to above, three canoes came to meet us. (I was then accompanied by another missionary). This was to do honor to us, to show respect and gratitude. When we approached near to the island two of these canoes were sent on ahead to announce to the king that we would arrive immediately, The king had all his braves armed (for they all have guns) and the moment we landed he commanded them to fire, after which he formed them into two lines and made them kneel to receive our benediction; they then rose and we passed between them. They accompanied us to the church where we chanted the Te Deum, or rather it was chanted by themselves in thanksgiving for our arrival. This is about the ordinary ceremony to honor the arrival of a missionary. When the mission was opened, after having implored the light of the Holy Spirit, they all confessed, and a great number received Holy Communion. I made the Stations of the Cross partly in their own Micmac language. I know that they understood me by the signs that they made, as well as by their devout appearance in following the procession. Afterwards each one came to make the Stations himself the best way he could. This went on for six days, during which time I left the pictures of the Stations in the church. I put a high indulgence on their crosses, crucifixes, beads, &c., by virtue of a power that I received from Rome since I came on this mission. Some Indians had given bad example and had openly sinned; these made public reparation, promising to correct themselves and praying the king, who was present in the church, to punish them, if they again fell into the same fault. I was obliged to leave, and had not time to erect fourteen large crosses which I had intended to place in the middle of the island to serve as a Calvary. They, themselves, made three crosses, probably by this time they have set them up (as I instructed them how to do) before leaving.

The Cape Breton Indians are the best of all the Micmacs, they are sober, obedient to their priests, exact in the observance of the smallest articles of religion (if indeed there be any small). It is true that they are ignorant, but this is pardonable in them because of the difficulty of their language. One day I had given Communion to an old squaw who was ill. They were all alarmed as she was not fasting when she received; they thought that both the priest and the squaw had been guilty of great disrespect to the Blessed Sacrament. In order to quiet them, I said to them in Micmac: "Kijidou," which means: "Be easy, there is no harm in that, it is permitted, I know what I have to do." Immediately they looked at each other and smiled, their consciences at rest. The missionary who was with me once said to them: "I want you to make me a road in the woods one or two miles long." The next day, very early in the morning, one or two hundred Indians, each armed with a hatchet, began to cut down the trees, and at the close of the day the road was finished. This incident alone will serve to illustrate their good will and devotion.

During the five years and a half in which I worked at the holy ministry in this second mission, I had consolations and God delivered me from many dangers besides those of which I have spoken. One winter when I went to one of the three Acadian parishes to hold a mission there, I fell between two large cakes of very thick ice; this was on the sea, for every winter in this part of the world the water freezes sufficiently to allow a man and even a horse and sleigh to pass over it. A young man with whom I was travelling, came to my assistance, and by his help, but more by the help of God, I drew myself out. I was safe, but very wet and benumbed with cold. Some days after I was seized with a violent sore throat, which I attributed to the accident that had happened to me a short time previously. Many times I have been on foot and on horseback night and day, going on sick calls in the most severe weather. I have walked upon the frozen sea on one day, and have passed the same place on the day following and seen that it would not then bear me, and should I have attempted to cross it then, I would have perished. When the navigation was open, almost all the journeys rendered necessary, by the wants of my people, I made by sea, sometimes going in a boat, sometimes in a larger vessel. Besides the general risk that one always runs on this perfidious element, I have often experienced bad weather and long and perilous passages, but the Lord has preserved me in the midst of the waters. I must not omit to mention a most critical moment when Monseigneur Plessis, Bishop of Quebec, with several other priests and myself were in danger of losing our lives in 1815, while going by sea to Chezzetcook, a parish situated twenty-one miles from Halifax, and of which I have already spoken. Monseigneur, two priests and myself, were in the same boat, we had just quitted a long boat that had brought us from the town to the harbor. We were about landing, but had still some breakers to avoid. Two totally unexperienced young Englishmen who were rowing us led us suddenly into grave danger. The sea rose very high, and we found ourselves crossing the breakers, so that we momentarily expected to have our boat upset and ourselves sent head over heels into the midst of the waters. All who saw us, or knew of our situation, thought that we ran the greatest risk; but we held on, thanks to Providence, who arranges all, and nothing was lost but my hat, which was struck by a breaker and carried into the sea. Not only has divine Providence often delivered me in like dangers that I can call to mind, but also we were protected in the tempest which we experienced in the beginning of December, 1823, when we were coming from America to France. If I have been exposed to danger on the sea, I have also on land, but God made the elements; He dwells therein, He is their master. I have fallen three times from the back of a horse, at great risk of being killed or of breaking a limb, and I have twice been robbed by thieves who broke into the house in which I usually resided; they took the little money I had, my clothes, etc., but I was absent from home when they executed their evil deed. God permitted it, may His holy name be blessed!

There are in the parish of Tracadie and its environs twenty or thirty-six families of negroes, of whom the greater number are Protestants. Besides being heretics they are rascals, given to all kinds of vice. I have often visited them, and upon every occasion that offered, tried to instruct them in spite of the danger that I ran of being ill-treated and perhaps killed by them, for there are some among them who are bad at heart and capable of evil deeds. I had some experience of this when I lived near them.

Recently one of these negroes, remarkable among the others for his age and his pretended learning, fell ill. I went to see him thinking that my visit would not displease him. There were a number of blacks round his bed, who were singing hymns and praying. They offered me a chair. I seated myself near the sick man and commenced to speak to him of death, of judgment and of the truth faith, of the only true religion in which we can save ourselves. Finally I said to him that he would be dammed if he died in his false belief. At these words the other negroes turned on me with fury; by their animated features, by their eyes flashing with anger, and by their horrible cries, I knew that I was not safe with them, and that I could do no good there, so I left the house. They followed me, crying out against the priests. A young ecclesiastic who accompanied me was very frightened, and I myself expected to be assaulted by them. There was one in particular more enraged than the others, and who screamed most loudly. He said that if a hundred or a thousand priests should speak to him of religion he would not believe one of them. I returned there some days afterwards with another priest who was conversant with English (for the sick man could not speak French). After some hours conversation with the missionary, the sick man asked him if he would come to him again when he sent for him. Soon after this I left the country, but I have reason to think that he sent for me. I do not know what is the result for his soul, whether he is converted or whether he remains in error, for the above incident occurred just before my return to France.

During the five years and a half that I have spent at Tracadie, which is in Nova Scotia, I have had the consolation of seeing four or five families of these Protestant negroes embrace the Catholic religion. Many other persons also of different nations and sects have changed their faith, to the great edification of the children of the true Church.

It has been found necessary to build new churches and to enlarge others, to enable them to hold their congregations, which have so increased in number, either by conversions, by the multiplying of the old Catholic families, or by the number of strangers who came every day to settle in this country, and who bring the true faith with them. For some time I was the only missionary there, and obliged to traverse forty or fifty leagues by land and by sea. I found every where colonies who were Catholic, as well as many persons who were not. If some zealous priests would go to carry spiritual help to all these people who are in a measure abandoned, they would perform a great act of charity and win much merit; but they must be prepared to suffer many miseries, hunger, cold, persecution, poverty, &c, and to risk their lives often both on land and sea. The principal nourishment of the people of the country consists of potatoes and salt meat, water or spruce beer (biere de Pruche) is their ordinary drink. They love rum which is common enough, and is not expensive— but on the other hand it is dangerous and unhealthful to soul and body. A very small quantity of this liquor will make a man lose his reason, and quite inebriate him. It is this unhappy and deadly drink that ruins the Indians in this country as in all others.

The climate of Nova Scotia and of Cape Breton is very cold during the winter (which lasts six months), and sometimes very hot in summer. From time to time we hear of persons having their hands and feet frozen, and even parts of their faces. I myself have seen many who were obliged to have their hands or feet amputated, they having mortified from the effects of the cold. Another danger that one has to face is that of being surrounded by the snow when it is drifted by the wind, as sometimes happens on the Alps, on the side of Mont Cenis and Simplon. This is what is called a "snow storm." In these eddies of snow one cannot see the road on which to travel, not even a house fifteen feet distant The snow, driven with force by the wind, fills your eyes, nostrils and mouth, and prevents you from breathing, so that you are really in danger of perishing. Every winter a tremendous quantity of snow falls, so that one is obliged to use snow-shoes in order to travel. In spite of all these drawbacks it is a healthy country, and one which produces all necessary grain and vegetables, such as wheat, bearded wheat, rye, kidney beans, beans, turnips, cabbage, potatoes, &c, and even good fruit, such as apples, pears and plums. As to the fruit, in some townships it is very good, in others it is small, while as to vegetables, potatoes succeed the best. These latter are very fine in Nova Scotia and in Cape Breton.

A proof of the country not being a bad one is, that every one lives well there. Strictly speaking, there are no poor, for one never sees a beggar. It has been remarked that those who work well, and are rather industrious, live in comfort, without being exactly rich. Again, the people have fish at their doors, for living as they do near the sea and the lakes, they can have all kinds, such as herring, mackerel, salmon, eels and codfish in abundance. It is true that the winter is long and severe, but there is plenty of wood with which to keep warm.

A consideration that ought to overweigh all the troubles and dangers which have been mentioned, is the great work that may be here done for religion among so many souls that are abandoned and given over to ignorance for want of priests to instruct them. More particularly among the Indian people, who deserve that we should try to save them, because of their good faith and fine natural character. It occurred to me to group them into villages as soon as I got to know them well; for that purpose I have bought a large tract of land near the sea, there to form a religious establishment which will serve to civilize them and to make them still better Christians. They will establish themselves near us, and we will be at hand to see them and to instruct them. I have built a house on this land, hoping that the Government or some charitable and generous soul will assist in erecting a chapel and some other buildings, that we shall need, in order to carry out our project, and to effect the good that we hope for. My Superior consents, and encourages me to return to America for this laudable undertaking, and in order to work for the salvation of those Indians who know not God, such as the Esquimaux. These latter are a barbarous and cannibalistic people. Recently they made a descent on some European fisherman in the woods that they inhabit, which are not far from the banks of Newfoundland, a little to the north. The Indians having let fly several arrows at the fishermen, the latter replied by some shots from their guns. One of the Indians was killed, the others saved themselves by flight. Our fishermen seized a squaw who remained near the dead body of the Indian; probably they had lived together, and she regarded him as her husband. She was taken to St John's Newfoundland, and the Governor having been notified gave orders to the merchants of the town to allow this Indian woman such wearing material as pleased her. It was noticed that she fancied everything of the most gaudy description. The colors, red in particular, pleased and delighted her, consequently the material she chose was principally red. They prepared something for her to eat and offered her food which had been cooked; she, however, scorned that, and seized upon a raw fowl which she devoured without removing the feathers. A Frenchman who was there and saw her, told me that her nails and teeth were extremely long. Instead of keeping her among civilized beings, she was taken to the woods where she had been found. This was probably by order of the Governor. It is very difficult to civilize this kind of Indian. They are very fierce, and their language, which is not the same as that of the Micmacs, seems to present great difficulties. Still these souls have been created by God and bought by Jesus Christ, and the more abandoned, and the further from the religion of heaven they seem to be, so much the more do they call for our compassion. We have succeeded in civilizing many barbarous nations and in rendering them Christian and Catholic, we may equally, with the help of God, bring others to the knowledge of the true religion, and since pretended philosophers have abandoned the faith, it must, according to the divine oracle, go to other men. If this faith is extinguished for many, who have deserved the misfortune in closing their eyes to its light, it goes to others who will render themselves worthy by allowing this divine truth to enlighten them. Thus faith is never lost, if it leaves us, it is our own fault.

To return to our Micmacs of Nova Scotia,—it does one good to reflect on what they were formerly and what they are now. Formerly they were ferocious idolaters, now they are gentle and they know the true God. If the Government had chosen to help us we could have done for the Esquimaux what the early missionaries did for the people of which we speak; and even these latter for whom we have worked would, without doubt, have become much more civilized. We would have ventured to promise to make of them, not only well instructed and perfect Christians, but also good laborers and good workmen, in a word, good citizens who would be useful to society and not a burden to the State as they have hitherto been. The way in which they have profited by the few lessons that they have received from us on agriculture is a proof of the success that we should have had. We have worked with them and our example has encouraged them. It is well that they know how to farm a little, for instance, how to plant potatoes, for the country is beginning to be populous, and they do not find enough game to subsist upon, and there are times when they cannot fish. It is then charitable as well as necessary to teach them to gain their livelihood in some other way. But all that is only a small part of the good that we propose to do; to work efficaciously at the saving of their souls, to render them humble, sober, industrious, charitable, &c., from religious principles which is the way by which we hope to complete and perfect the good work. Not having succeeded so far in making an establishment of any consequence, by reason of want of means, we have contented ourselves with forming a little school for girls, more especially for the young Micmac squaws. This school is taught by three excellent women, natives of the place, who live as religious of the third order of La Trappe, until such time as they can establish a house of the first order. They have already gone through a year of novitiate at the convent of the Ladies of the Congregation of Montreal, in Canada, which congregation was founded by Sister Bourgeoys, as one reads in the history of the discovery of that great country. These three women are stationed in the parish of Pomquete, one of the three parishes with which I am especially charged, and of which mention has been made at the beginning of this narrative. It is a good little parish, composed of French people, born most of them at St Malo, Dinan or Grandville. When I left these poor people in order to return to France, they were inconsolable, fearing they would have no priest. They called a meeting to discuss what they should do in the event of so sad a situation. Many were resolved to follow me with the hope of bringing me back, or of returning with another priest. All were agreed to pay the passage of the missionary who should come to them, as well as to undertake to supply all that might be necessary for food or raiment while he should be with them. One man named Dominique Phillippar, born in Paris, and a resident of Pomquett for about thirty years, was chosen for an important errand. He was to accompany me to France, and to entreat the Reverend Father Abbot, my Superior, that I or some other member of our Order might return with him. In case that could not be managed, we were by his recommendation and through his instrumentality to address ourselves to the Bishop, asking for some zealous priests who were willing to consecrate themselves to the North American missions, and to minister to people who had no spiritual help. His place was secured in the ship that took me to France, but as he had not arrived from his parish when we set sail, he lost his passage, the ship having sailed a day earlier than was expected. Doubtless the good man experienced poignant regret. He was ready to journey almost two thousand leagues (including going and coming) in order to get a priest. This fact illustrates the faith and zeal for religion existing in the Catholics of these countries. I hope that God who is often satisfied with our good will and who permitted this event, will inspire some good ecclesiastics with the desire of going to the aid of these poor souls who so well deserve assistance.

When we arrived in America we found most Catholics well disposed. Their religion was obscured, but they seemed to be impressed with the first invitations or instructions that we gave them; of this they gave exterior proof, such as building churches, erecting crosses on the roadside, establishing Calvaries, and making the way of the cross, a devotion which touches the heart and bears excellent fruit. I, myself, have often been witness of the good effect produced by the Stations, and it is not long since one of my parishoners who was given over to drunkenness was completely converted after assisting at this devotion. He threw himself at my feet dissolved in tears, made his confession, and since that time he has always been extremely sober and filled with the fear of God. I often make the Stations in the different places where I go to hold missions, and as I have remarked a change for the better in the manners and in the amusements, the dancing, vanities, &c, of the people, I attribute it to the grace attached to the devotion of the way of the cross.

Those who have resolved to go over to those countries will do well to procure the faculty for establishing this precious devotion everywhere.

Ut in nomine Jesu omne genu flectatur caelestium, terrestrium et infernorum. Ad Philippenses, 2 10.

"At the name of Jesus every knee shall bow, whether in heaven, or on earth, or in hell."

[Footnote: The Procession of the most Holy Sacrament made by the Indians of Cape Breton and the Bras d'Or has not been mentioned in these pages, as it took place since this narrative was written.]

* * * * *

TRANSLATOR'S NOTE.

The foregoing very imperfect translation of Father Vincent de Paul's quaint narrative, is published at the request of the leading clergy of Antigonish County, that section of Eastern Nova Scotia in which the holy Trappist so long lived and labored.

The original from which the translation was made, was printed in France in the year 1824, and, as far as is known, is the only copy in Canada. It was for many years lying perdu in the old convent of the Trappistine Sisters, in Tracadie, Nova Scotia, where it was discovered in the autumn of 1883. It is interspersed with corrections and footnotes in the pious monk's own handwriting and was printed at a private press, in the Trappist Monastery at Bellefontaine, France.

Father Vincent's labors were, generally speaking, confined to the district over which he presided, but occasionally in cases of urgent need, he would be sent for to administer the Sacraments to the dying in Prince Edward Island. Old Catholic residents along the northern and eastern shores of King's County, will tell how, with Father Vincent seated in the prow, the smallest boat would ride safely over an angry sea.

His apostolic zeal it was that kept the Faith alive in Eastern Nova Scotia, in the days when, with the exception of a few French missions, it lived only in the hearts of the poor Micmac Indians. Before his death, however, he had the happiness of seeing the

Catholic religion firmly rooted in the land he so loved, by the arrival and establishment there of the loyal Highlanders, who by their energy and perseverance have changed the desert through which Father Vincent made his perilous journeys into a beautiful and fertile country.

To the Right Rev. Dr. Cameron for his kindness in writing the preface, to the Rev. Clergy for their liberal patronage, and to the Trappistine Sisters for the loan of the original copy of Father Vincent's book, are due the most grateful thanks of

THE TRANSLATOR.
Charlottetown, P.E. Island, 18th June, 1886.

.

www.ingramcontent.com/pod-product-compliance
Lightning Source LLC
Chambersburg PA
CBHW030815090426
42737CB00010B/1286